IT'S MY LIFE!

S.A.I.N.

By: Stephen and Susan Nagy with the love and guidance of
Gabrielle, Timothy and Jack

WestBow·
PRESS
A DIVISION OF THOMAS NELSON
& ZONDERVAN

WestBow Press books may be ordered through booksellers or by contacting:

WestBow Press
A Division of Thomas Nelson & Zondervan
1663 Liberty Drive
Bloomington, IN 47403
www.westbowpress.com
1 (866) 928-1240

Because of the dynamic nature of the Internet, any web addresses or links contained in this book may have changed since publication and may no longer be valid. The views expressed in this work are solely those of the author and do not necessarily reflect the views of the publisher, and the publisher hereby disclaims any responsibility for them.

Any people depicted in stock imagery provided by Thinkstock are models, and such images are being used for illustrative purposes only.
Certain stock imagery © Thinkstock.

ISBN: 978-1-4908-7404-3 (sc)
ISBN: 978-1-4908-7405-0 (e)

Library of Congress Control Number: 2015904332

Print information available on the last page.

WestBow Press rev. date: 4/3/2015

SEARCH YOUR SOUL

SAVE YOUR SOUL

SEEK YOUR SOUL

Exodus 3:14

"And God said unto Moses,

I AM THAT I AM:

and he said,

Thus shalt thou say unto the children of Israel,

I AM

hath sent me unto you."

I AM

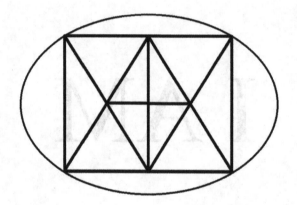

THANK YOU LORD

Thank you Lord for my eyes, nose, mouth & voice, for my ears, hands, feet, heart & mind.

Thank you Lord for my body, soul & dreams, for my prayers, your love & time.

Thank you Lord for my Eyes that I might see, all on earth and in the skies up above.

Thank you Lord for my Nose that I might smell and breathe the air provided through your Love.

Thank you Lord for my Mouth that I might taste and greet the world with my smile.

Thank you Lord for my Voice that I might speak and share my thoughts awhile.

Thank you Lord for my Ears that I might hear all the sounds and words in the air.

Thank you Lord for my Hands that I might feel and lend a hand everywhere.

Thank you Lord for my Feet that I might walk wherever you need me to be.

Thank you Lord for my Heart that I might share the love you share with me.

Thank you Lord for my Mind that I might learn the lessons of my life.

Thank you Lord for my Body's health and strength and Soul showing your true light.

Thank you Lord for the Dreams you let me share with my friends and with my family.

Thank you Lord for the Prayers you use to share your guiding light with me.

Thank you Lord for the Love you let me share with my friends and with my enemies.

Thank you Lord for the Time you let me share with you through eternity.

Thank you Lord for these Gifts that I might know how blessed I am while on earth.

Thank you Lord for the Days you've let me share your goodness since my birth.

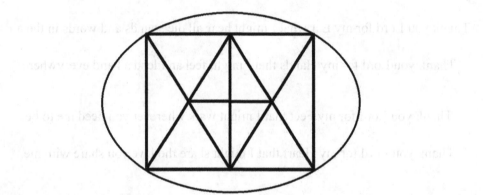

Thank you, Lord for another beautiful day here on earth
and thank you for everything that you have given me.

Thank you for all the blessings you've bestowed on me,
for all the love you have shown me and for
all the gifts that you have given me.

Thank you especially for

....

Thank you for my EYES that I might see everything in the world around me and in the skies up above.

My eyes have seen:	I would love to see:

Thank you for my NOSE that I might smell all the aromas that come my way and that I might breathe the air that you provide for me to breathe.

My nose has smelled:	I would love to smell:

Thank you for my MOUTH that I might taste all the tastes that come my way and that I might express the feelings that I have within me.

My mouth has tasted:	I would love to taste:

My mouth has expressed:	I would love to express:

Thank you for my VOICE that I might give glory, thanks and praise to you, O Lord and that I might communicate with others here on earth.

Thoughts my voice has spoken:	Thoughts I would love to share:

Thank you for my EARS that I might hear all the sounds
that there are to hear, that I might hear the words spoken
to me by others and that I might hear your words Lord
and do your will accordingly here on earth.

My ears have heard:	I would love to hear:

Thank you for my HANDS that I might feel all the things that I touch and that I might lend a helping hand whenever it is needed.

My hands have felt:	I would love to feel:
Ways my hands have helped others:	Ways I would love to use my hands to help:

Thank you for my FEET for they give me the mobility to get to the places where you need me to do your will here on earth.

My feet have taken me to:	I would love my feet to take me to:

Thank you for my HEART, help me to show all
the love that you have given me to others.

My heart has shown love to:	I would love to show love to:

Thank you for my MIND that I might grow in wisdom
and understanding with each passing day.

My mind has learned:	I would love to learn:

Thank you for my BODY, help me to keep it healthy and strong.

My body has been healthy and strong in the following ways:	I would love to keep my body healthy and strong in the following ways:

Thank you for my SOUL, help me to make your light
within me shine forth for all the world to see.

My soul has shined forth through:	I would love my soul to shine forth through:

Thank you Lord, for the DREAMS you let me share with my friends and with my family that bring Hope.

Dreams I have shared:	Dreams I would love to share:

Thank you Lord, for the PRAYERS you use to share your guiding light with me that increase my Faith.

Guidance I have received:	Guidance I would love:

Thank you Lord, for the LOVE you let me share
with my friends and with my enemies.

Friends & Enemies I have shared Love with:	Friends and Enemies I need to Love:

Thank you Lord, for the TIME you let me
share with you through eternity.

Time that I have shared with God:	Time that I would love to share with God:

Lord, THANK YOU for all these gifts, help me to do your will here on earth – today and everyday – help me to make good decisions and to accomplish the tasks that I need to accomplish so that your will may be done here on earth.

LORD, I ASK YOU THESE THINGS, IN THE
NAME OF THE FATHER, AND OF THE SON,
AND OF THE HOLY SPIRIT, AMEN.

Count Your Blessings

Sight

Smell

Taste

Voice

Sound

Touch

Movement

Heart – (Emotional Being)

Mind – (Intellectual Being)

Body – (Physical Being)

Soul – (Spiritual Being)

Dreams

Prayers

Love

Time

GRATITUDE

When we take a moment to appreciate this, we can make the... so can begin to appreciate the gifts that each of us have given by God. When we do this, truly recognize and appreciate these gifts as our resources, we can then develop and implement an action plan in which we CHANGE our outlook to positive. When we gain a positive outlook, we obtain the confidence necessary to accomplish the goals that we set for ourselves.

When we identify what we would love to do, we can then love our life. For only we can determine what we wish our life on earth to be.

Now that I have invested the time to search my soul, I can identify the resources that I have been given and give thanks for those resources.

(Giving thanks will give me a positive attitude!)

My next step is to define my dream and how I can make it MY LIFE.

IT'S MY LIFE PLAN

Whenever we take a moment to enjoy the beauty that surrounds us, we can begin to appreciate the gifts that we have been given by God. When we take this time to recognize and appreciate these gifts as our resources, we can then develop and implement an action plan in which we CHANGE our outlook to positive. When we gain a positive outlook we obtain the confidence necessary to accomplish the goals that we set for ourselves.

When we identify what we would love to do, we can begin to love our life. For only we can determine what we wish our life on earth to be.

Now that I have invested the time to search my soul, I can identify the resources that I have been given and give thanks for these resources.

Giving thanks will give me a positive attitude!

My next step is to define my dream and how I can make it MY LIFE.

RESOURCES

MY DREAM

The TIME has come for all people to search their souls and identify their DREAMS. When we take this opportunity, we recognize the motivating forces of Faith, Hope and Love in our lives and utilize them to accomplish our DREAMS.

I PRAY that each individual will recognize that we are all created equal in GOD's likeness and that TIME is the equalizing factor in our lives. The resource of TIME must be managed to its fullest potential. Give THANKS to GOD for each minute of our life and ask for his wisdom to use it wisely.

My Dream is:

_____

_____

_____

_____

_____

_____

_____

_____

I Pray that this dream be known to God and all mankind on this _____day of _____ in the year of our Lord, _____. I pledge to myself and to all mankind to use my time on earth to work to make my dreams come true. Thank you.

Sincerely,

_____

MY PLAN

Now that I have defined MY DREAM, I need to develop MY action plan for the journey that will help me make the decisions I will face on MY journey of MY LIFE!

MY FIRST FIFTEEN STEPS

1) _____

_____

_____

_____

2) _____

_____

_____

_____

3) _____

_____

_____

_____

4) _____

_____

_____

_____

5) _____

_____

_____

_____

6)

7)

8)

9)

10)

11) _____

_____

_____

_____

12) _____

_____

_____

_____

13) _____

_____

_____

_____

14) _____

_____

_____

_____

15) _____

_____

_____

_____